TOP GEAR

THE HISTORY OF AUTOMOBILES

Peter Lafferty and David Jefferis

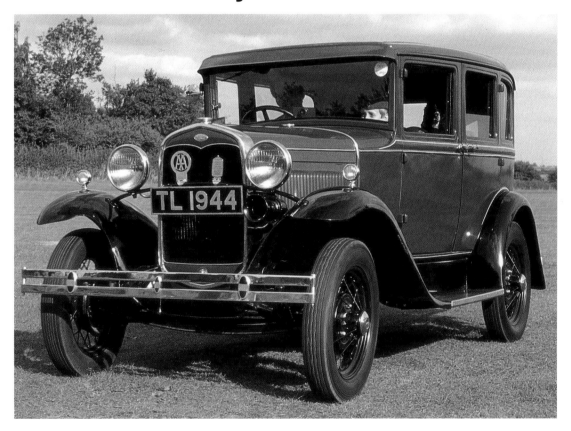

Franklin Watts

New York London Toronto Sydney

Illustrated by
Robert Burns
Chris Forsey
Ron Jobson
Michael Roffe

Photographs supplied by
Mary Evans Picture Library
Ferrari F40 by
kind permission,
Maranello Concessionaires
David Jefferis
Mike Key
Rover Group

Technical consultant
Peter Dickinson,
Assistant Editor of
Volksworld magazine

© 1990 Franklin Watts

Franklin Watts Inc.
387 Park Avenue South
New York, NY 10016

Printed in Belgium

Library of Congress Cataloging-in-Publication
Data

Lafferty, Peter.
Top gear : the story of automobile / Peter Lafferty
and David Jefferis.
p. cm. – – (Wheels)
Summary: Discusses the pioneers in automotive
history and the evolution of different types of cars.
ISBN 0–531–14038–5
1. Automobiles—History—Juvenile literature.
[1. Motorcycles—History.] I. Jefferis. David.
II. Title. III. Series: Lafferty, Peter. Wheels.
TL147.L33 1990
629.222—dc20   89–21535
                                                    CIP
                                                    AC

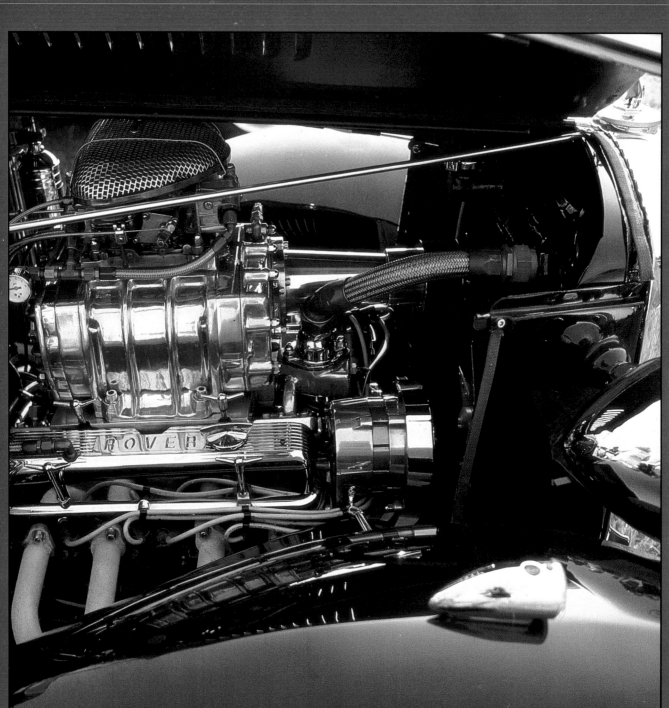

TOP GEAR

Contents

Introduction

The age of the automobile began in October 1885 when the first car lurched forward, threw its German inventor Karl Benz out of the driving seat, then crashed into a wall.

Despite this poor start, Benz carried on with his vehicle and in a few years he and others were making cars for sale to the public. There was some resistance at first. Many people thought the new vehicles were smelly, dangerous and expensive. But as new types of car were developed, they became cheaper and more reliable.

Today, the enthusiasm of the motoring public has meant there are 400 million or so automobiles in the world. The car has become a victim of its own success though, with huge problems of pollution, congestion and road safety.

The first cars were very different from those of today. The 1885 Benz was a three-wheeler with its engine below the driver's seat. The vehicle had just three wire-spoked wheels and was mostly made of metal tubing. It was steered by a tiller rather than a steering wheel. The engine drove the back wheels by a chain rather than today's rods and gears. Driving the Benz was an outdoors job as it had no enclosed bodywork. The driver sat high up, exposed to wind and weather. The wheels had solid rubber tires which gave a hard and bumpy ride. Top speed was about 14 kilometers per hour (9 mph).

A modern car, such as the Porsche 959, shows how far the car maker's art has progressed. The Porsche is one of the fastest road vehicles, with a top speed over 317 km/h (197 mph). The smooth, streamlined shape of the metal and plastic body helps the car push through the air with little resistance or drag.

The Porsche is unusual for its rear-mounted engine, as most modern cars have engines at the front. Power is fed to all four wheels. This makes the 959 safer to drive on slippery roads than conventional two-wheel-drive models.

▷ There are three basic engine positions. A car handles best if its engine is mid-mounted between the front and rear wheels like the Ferrari shown here. Front-mounted engines are most common, as this arrangement allows more room inside.

Less often, cars have rear-mounted engines. Cars like this can have cornering problems though – the engine weight tends to push the rear into a skid.

Old and new — a century of progress

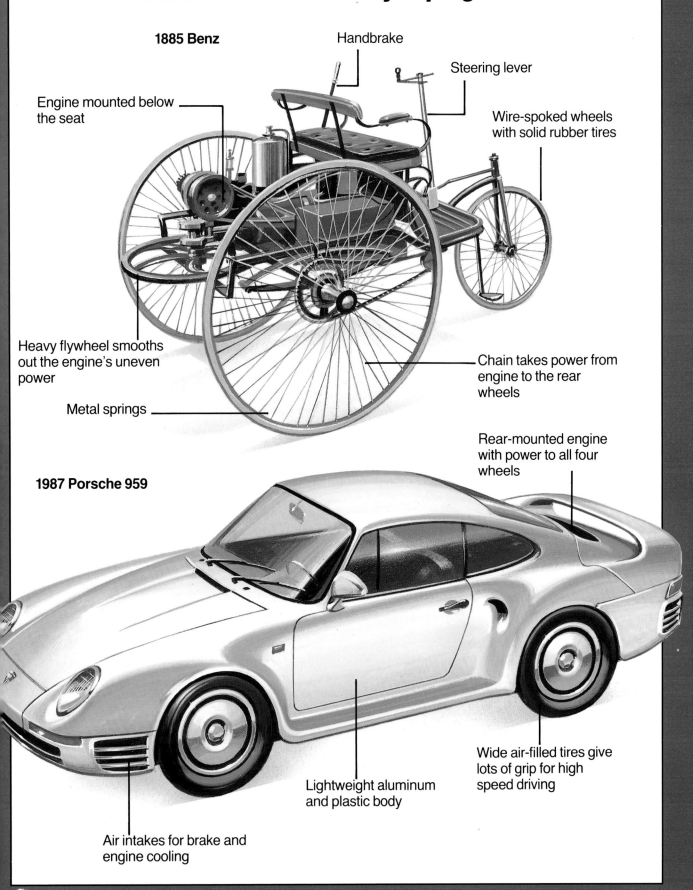

1885 Benz

Handbrake

Steering lever

Engine mounted below the seat

Wire-spoked wheels with solid rubber tires

Heavy flywheel smooths out the engine's uneven power

Chain takes power from engine to the rear wheels

Metal springs

Rear-mounted engine with power to all four wheels

1987 Porsche 959

Lightweight aluminum and plastic body

Wide air-filled tires give lots of grip for high speed driving

Air intakes for brake and engine cooling

The power of steam

Over a century before Karl Benz's three wheeler, engineers were experimenting with self-propelled vehicles. These did not have gasoline-fueled engines however, but were powered by steam.

In 1771, Frenchman Nicolas Cugnot built a sturdy three-wheel steam wagon. A water-filled copper boiler at the front was heated to make steam. The hot steam was piped into a pair of hollow tubes, called cylinders, astride the front wheel. Inside each cylinder a piston was pushed up and down by the pressure of the steam. The movement of the pistons turned the front wheel.

Cugnot's steam wagon was intended to pull heavy guns for the French army, a job normally reserved for horses or oxen. Unfortunately, the wagon ran out of steam every 12 minutes or so, and it had to stop to have its boiler topped up with water. Also, the machine was difficult to steer, and on its first run in Paris, France, it caused the first motor accident by going out of control and smashing into a stone wall at 3 km/h (2 mph). The army officers watching the demonstration were not impressed and the wagon was never used as a gun carrier.

Later, more successful steam vehicles were built. On Christmas Eve, 1801, Richard Trevithick drove his steam carriage up a hill near Camborne,

△ Cugnot's steam wagon, making history by smashing into a wall. The vehicle's heavy boiler and front wheel assembly made steering the slow-moving machine difficult.

England. The carriage ran out of steam by the time it had puffed to the top, but coasted safely downhill back to town.

Four days later, Trevithick drove the carriage to his local inn, intending to enjoy a large meal. He parked the steamer in an outbuilding, but didn't douse the boiler fire. Sparks started a blaze and in minutes, both his carriage and the outbuilding were burned to ashes.

After this accident, Trevithick concentrated on building railroad locomotives. Most people lost interest in steam-powered road vehicles with the coming of the railroad. Steam locos running on metal rails could go faster and were less prone to accidents.

Steam cars

△ Despite many failures, successful steam road vehicles were eventually built. In 1883, a steam carriage called *Enterprise* was carrying passengers around London.

△ The best steam cars were the American Stanleys. In 1899, a Stanley steamer was driven up Mount Washington, in the state of New Hampshire. In 1906, Fred Marriott drove another Stanley, the *Wogglebug,* to an unofficial world record speed of 204 km/h (127 mph). An attempt to beat this the following year ended in disaster as the *Wogglebug* hit a bump and spun end over end. Roadgoing Stanley steamers were powerful, smooth and quiet. They were also difficult to start – it could take the best part of an hour to get up steam. The convenience of the gasoline engine marked the end of steam as competition.

The first cars

The age of the automobile really began with the invention of a new kind of engine to replace steam power. This was called the internal combustion engine because fuel was burned inside, rather than using an outside fire like the steamers. The earliest internal combustion engines burned gas made from coal. In 1864, Austrian engineer Siegfried Marcus fixed one of these engines to a wooden cart. He drove the cart a short way before it broke down.

The next development was made by a German, Nicolaus Otto. He developed an improved internal combustion engine which produced its power in four strokes,

△ Daimler's 1886 car was a horse coach with the shafts cut off. For this reason it was called a "horseless carriage." Like Benz's tricycle it had a tiller to steer with. The engine was under the back seat. The car could take four people at a steady 16 km/h (10 mph).

or movements, of the piston. However, Otto did not use his engine to drive an automobile because the gas fuel did not provide enough power. The development of the motor car was left to two other German engineers, Karl Benz and Gottlieb Daimler.

Benz and Daimler realized that gasoline, a liquid produced when crude petroleum oil is refined, was a more powerful fuel than coal gas. Around 1879, Benz built a working engine in his Mannheim workshop. He mounted this on a three-wheeled tricycle in 1885. The tricycle (shown in detail on page 5) crashed during its first test run, but it showed promise. The next trial was more successful as the machine spluttered jerkily along for some distance. Then came a run at 14 km/h (9 mph).

When the editor of the local newspaper heard the news, he was unimpressed however, saying "Who is interested in horseless carriages when there are horses for sale?"

Meanwhile, in the nearby town of Bad Cannstatt, Gottlieb Daimler was also experimenting. In 1886, he fitted a gasoline-fueled engine to a horse carriage, making the first four-wheeled car. Once again a local newspaper failed to see the point. After the first test run, the paper called the vehicle "diabolical and dangerous to life."

It was Karl Benz's wife, Bertha, who showed how useful her husband's invention could be. In 1888, she set out from Mannheim in the latest Benz car to visit relatives in Pforzheim, 100 km (60

miles) away. Her two sons, Eugen and Richard joined her on the journey.

Along the way they startled people, horses and other animals. In one village, a shoe maker nailed strips of leather onto the brake shoes. At another village, a hatpin was used to unblock a fuel pipe. Another time, Bertha had to tie an elastic garter onto an engine part to stop it from falling off. This journey was the first long distance trip by car. Today it would take less than an hour. It took Bertha, Eugen and Richard all day!

The Benz automobiles were leaders of the pack. Within a few years, dozens of car-makers were competing with new and improved machines. The first Benz car survives in a museum in Munich, Germany.

△ The Benz family stops for repairs on the day trip to Pforzheim. This machine could manage a speed of over 19 km/h (12 mph).

▽ Motoring accessories included ladies' hoods, men's traveling caps and warning horns like this to honk at pedestrians!

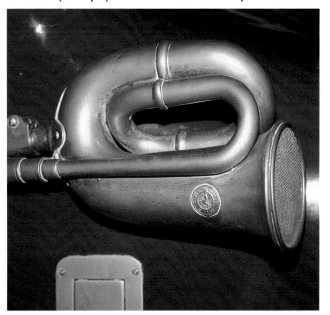

It's frightening the horses!

The coming of the motor car was not welcomed by everyone. Many people complained that cars were too dangerous and noisy to be used on the highways. In particular, horses were easily frightened by the new vehicles. In Germany and Britain, pioneer motorists were expected to stop for a horse, switch off the engine and help the animal past. It was against the law for a car to travel faster than a horse could trot.

Even so, accidents could easily happen. In 1894, the Swiss Count Cognard drove his Peugeot across the Alps into Italy, an amazing feat considering the mountainous terrain and Switzerland's speed limit of 6 km/h (4 mph). As the car roared through the Italian village of Ticino, an army officer's horse reared in terror, throwing its rider to the ground. Luckily he was only bruised, but was so annoyed that he telephoned ahead to the next village, ordering the police to arrest and fine the motorist. Luck was with the Count, however. The telephone did not work properly and the officer's orders were misheard. The Count was certainly stopped, but instead of being punished, he was given a room in the local hotel!

In 1897, a road accident nearly started a small war in Paris. Monsieur Hughes le Roux was knocked down by a car going, he said, "at the speed of an express train." Le Roux wrote to the Police Chief calling motorists "mad dogs," warning that in the future he planned to carry a pistol and shoot anyone he saw driving a car. Word of le Roux's threat got out and local motorists replied that if pedestrians were going to carry pistols, then car drivers would carry machine guns. For a while it looked as if war was going to break out between motorists and pedestrians!

Although it seems odd to be frightened of cars, today's accident rates would be considered completely unacceptable to a person of the nineteenth century.

▷ Minor battles between horseriders and motorists were not uncommon, and the Count's adventures were typical. Though speed limits were an early part of the motoring age, a law-breaking driver could outrun a horse-mounted policeman in a long chase. Tire technology was in its early stages, the first cars having wooden wheels with iron tires. The air-filled pneumatic tire was perfected in the 1890s. One of the first such tire designs was used in the 1,171 km (732 miles) Paris-Bordeaux race of 1894. The Michelin brothers used 22 new inner tubes during the race. They gave up after 90 hours due to the number of punctures! The race had been won by another competitor many hours before.

◁ British pioneer motorists were limited to 8 km/h (5 mph) in the country, 3 km/h (2 mph) in towns. Someone had to walk in front of the car waving a red flag to warn of the vehicle's approach. These restrictions had been introduced in the days of steam carriages. When the motorcar arrived, the restrictions were still enforced, though after 1878 the red flag was not needed.

A ghost on wheels

Henry Royce was an Englishman whose engineering firm, FH Royce and Company, made rugged and reliable machines including dynamos and cranes. His high standards led him to make a car that many people felt was the best in the world.

In 1903, Royce bought his first car, a French Decauville. It went reasonably well, but it was noisy and poorly made. Royce was sure he could do better and began building a quieter, more reliable machine. On April 1, 1904, his first experimental automobile was ready for the highway. The car ran perfectly on its first run, and a month later the machine impressed Charles Rolls, an aristocratic sportsman. After a demonstration by Royce, the two men agreed to make and sell cars under the name Rolls-Royce, with Rolls' associate, Claude Johnson, adding business flair to the partnership.

The first really great Rolls-Royce car was the Silver Ghost, launched as the 40/50 model in 1906. It was made to the highest standards, regardless of cost. Where necessary, parts were polished and examined under a magnifying glass to detect flaws. The result was a car that ran so silently it made "no more noise than a ghost." Some of the early cars actually had silver plated parts, so truly lived up to their name.

The Silver Ghost won its reputation as best car in the world because of its reliability, luxury and attention to detail. It stayed in production, a worldwide symbol of quality, for nearly 20 years.

In 1912, a Silver Ghost took part in a hill climbing test in the Austrian Alps. To the intense shame of Henry Royce, the car failed the test because the gearbox was not strong enough. The box was modified and the car was entered for the following year's competition. This time, it won full marks. Tests like this helped establish Rolls-Royce as a leading carmaker.

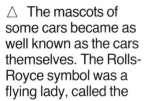

△ The mascots of some cars became as well known as the cars themselves. The Rolls-Royce symbol was a flying lady, called the "spirit of ecstasy."

The three-pointed star was adopted by Mercedes-Benz after Gottlieb Daimler, one of the firm's founders, wrote, "one day a star will arise to recognize my work."

The winged B was used by Bentley, a high-quality carmaker. The firm was bought by Rolls-Royce in 1931, but Bentleys are still made and sold as very expensive and very luxurious sports cars.

Cars by the million

Henry Ford was an American engineer and businessman who made the first inexpensive cars. Unlike Rolls-Royce, which produced a few cars that were built to perfection but with a price to match, Ford aimed to make cars at a price anyone could afford.

His first car had one flaw though. He had forgotten to install a reverse gear and had to push it from its garage! There were no such design mistakes in his 1908 Ford Model T. The "Tin Lizzie" (available in black only, as offering a color choice would slow production down) went on to sell in its millions.

To make cheap cars, Ford had to abandon the methods used by other car makers. Rolls-Royce used engineer-craftsmen who lovingly hand-assembled, tested and polished each part – tasks which took a long time. Ford changed all that and pioneered the method still used today – mass production.

The work of building a car was split up into a number of different jobs with each worker concentrating on one thing. Finished items were added to the partly-built cars as they moved slowly along a conveyor belt called the production line. Car bodies were assembled on one line. The base structure, including chassis, engine and wheels on another. When finished, bodies passed down a sloping platform onto the completed running gear. At the line's end, the finished cars were started up and driven off. At the peak of the Model T's popularity, a car could be assembled in just over an hour. The Model T sold until 1927, when over 15 million had been made.

△ The Tin Lizzie was made in a variety of body styles, including this four-seater with removable top.

▷ Horses and motorized vehicles shared city streets in the early 1900s. This 1910 photograph shows a busy scene as a horse-drawn carriage and motor-bus go about their business.

◁ Car bodies meet wheels, chassis and engine in the Ford plant at Detroit. Cars made by mass-production could be assembled ten times quicker than those made by old methods.

Speed demons

Drivers have been trying to break records since the dawn of motoring. Among the biggest challenges has been the World Land Speed Record. To gain the title, drivers have to make two straight runs along a "flying mile" (1.6 km), with space to start and stop at either end. Runs are measured, one each way, to allow for wind direction and the average of both attempts is the official speed.

Among the first Land Speed Record holders was Belgian Camille Jenatzy, known as the "Red Devil" because of his large red beard. In 1899, excited spectators watched as his cigar-shaped car *La Jamais Contente* (Never Satisfied) hurtled along a track in Achères park, near Paris. With a thin whine from its electric motors, the car tore along at a record breaking 106 km/h (65 mph). There were fears that Jenatzy would not be able to breathe at this amazing speed, but all was well. The spectators could not guess, of course, that cars would one day travel at more than ten times this speed.

Today record speeds are in various groups, for wheel-driven, rocket and jet cars. Englishman Richard Noble held the record for jet-propelled cars for most of the 1980s. On October 4, 1983, he reached 1,019 km/h (633 mph) in his car *Thrust 2.* The gold colored machine made its runs across the mud flats at Black Rock desert in Nevada.

An even higher speed was achieved in 1979 by American Stan Barrett in his rocket-powered *Budweiser Rocket.* He reached 1,190 km/h (740 mph), faster than the speed of sound. Unfortunately, the timing equipment was not accurate enough, so his supersonic run could not count for the official world record.

▷ *Thrust 2* was specially built to beat the land speed record. The car was powered by a jet engine normally used in fighter aircraft.

Richard Noble sat beside the engine in a steel protected cockpit. The vehicle ran on solid aluminum wheels as rubber tires would rip apart instantly at record-breaking speeds. Parachutes helped to slow the car down after each high-speed run.

Challengers old and new

Nearly a century separates these two record machines. Both represent the peak of speed and power for their time.

The bullet-shaped car *La Jamais Contente* was electric powered, as were many of the early record breakers. Batteries supplied electricity to the motors.

Jenatzy's car held the speed record until 1902, when a steam car hurtled along at 120 km/h (75 mph).

In the 1980s, an exact replica of *La Jamais Contente* was built, and in 1989 the new machine was driven at 112 km/h (70 mph), beating Jenatzy's speed.

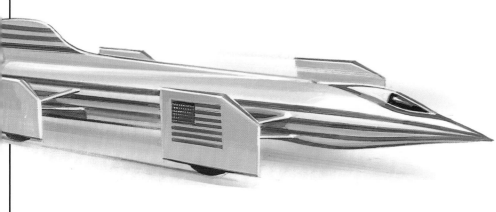

◁ Rocket power is Bill Gaynor's choice for his Project 1000 machine. Seven rocket units are designed to take the car *City of Sterling* to a top speed of over 1,600 km/h (1,000 mph) in 24 seconds from a standing start.

An ejection capsule is provided for Gaynor to make an escape in case of emergency at speed.

People's cars

In 1937, Austrian engineer Ferdinand Porsche produced an odd-looking car. The humpy machine looked more like an insect . . . a beetle! But Porsche had included various advanced features in his new design, including an air-cooled engine at the rear and an efficient suspension system. It was not until 1945, after the end of World War II, that full-scale production of Porsche's vehicle got underway. The Volkswagen or "people's car" went on to become the most popular car of all time. By 1987, over 21 million Beetles had been made.

The Beetle was strong and reliable, and because of this, many remarkable feats were undertaken in the car, including a drive across Australia's Stony Desert, one of the hottest places on Earth. In Antarctica, a Beetle survived sub-zero temperatures to provide transport for a research team.

Successful as the Beetle was, its layout was not as efficient as a British competitor, the 1959 Mini, designed by Alec Issigonis. The Mini had a sideways mounted front engine, driving the front wheels. This layout packed all the drive components into a small space, releasing more room for driver and passengers. The layout also gave the Mini good roadholding and the little car was driven to success in many 1960s rallies.

Like almost all modern cars, the Mini has unit construction. Most early cars, including the Beetle, had a separate chassis which formed the vehicle's "backbone," to which various parts (engine, wheels, body and so on) were attached. Unitary construction uses the body as a lightweight but strong box, replacing the heavy chassis.

◁ Today, early Beetles are highly collectable, and the open-top cabriolet model is the most prized of all.

▷ The Mini was a very successful rally car in the 1960s. It was able to cope with all terrain, from snowy Sweden to dusty Africa.

Best-selling front drivers

Today's best sellers are all based on the front-drive package pioneered by the Mini. Millions of front-drive cars are sold every year.

Fiat Uno (Italy)

Toyota Corolla (Japan)

VW Golf (Germany)

Ferrari!

The red Ferrari car is Italy's symbol of ultimate high performance. The man behind the car was Enzo Ferrari.

Young Enzo was fascinated by cars. He saw his first race in 1908 when he was ten and decided to become a racing driver. Three years later he had learned to drive and in 1919 joined the firm of CMN as a test and delivery driver. He raced several times for CMN, but soon was driving for Alfa Romeo, and in October 1920 he finished second in the Targa Floria race.

He was a good driver, but not outstanding. He was better as a manager and in the 1930s he had his own racing team, the Scuderia Ferrari. By the 1950s, Ferrari was making road cars as well, mostly painted blood-red and all decorated with Ferrari's prancing horse emblem.

To celebrate 40 years in business, the F40 was produced in 1987. It was the first road car capable of 320 km/h (201 mph). Enzo Ferrari died a year later and today his firm is owned by the giant Italian Fiat company. Developing new vehicles is expensive and, like many other small makers, Ferrari had to get the financial support of a big firm in order to continue making cars.

The big auto makers make their money from producing "bread and butter" cars for mass production. But having a sports car adds prestige, so the big firms are usually eager to buy sports car makers when they get the chance.

▷ In 1923, Enzo Ferrari won an important motor race in Ravenna, Italy. In honor of his performance, the parents of Francesco Baracca, a famous Italian fighter pilot of World War I, gave Ferrari a present. It was a piece of their son's plane, bearing a black prancing horse.

Ferrari adopted the emblem, though it did not appear on his cars until the Spa 24 hour race in July 1932.

At this race, Ferrari's cars finished first and second. The lucky horse has been used as the Ferrari symbol ever since.

△ The Chevrolet Corvette ZR-1 is the "king of the hill" car from the world's largest auto group, General Motors. The Corvette first came out in the 1950s and has been updated ever since.

▽ Among Ferrari's rivals in the supercar league is the German firm of BMW. This is the BMW 8-series, a powerful car electronically controlled to a maximum speed of 250 km/h (155 mph).

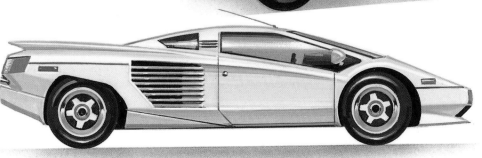

◁ The mid-engined Cizeta-Moroda V16T is a rival in speed and power to the top Ferraris. Inside, the V16T cocoons its driver and passenger in leather-lined luxury.

21

Eastern dawn

In 1956, Japan's motor industry exported just 46 cars to other countries. Today, over 3.5 million Japanese cars are exported every year and many more are made in Japanese-owned factories situated around the world.

Japan's success is remarkable considering that many of the country's factories were bombed flat during World War II. After the war, new factories were built using high-tech machines to make vehicles very efficiently. These, along with a high level of reliability and design and sales skills, have ensured spectacular success – today's Japanese motor industry is beaten in size only by that of the United States, and Toyota is the world's biggest individual car maker. However, all the world's auto makers now face an uncertain future.

Making huge numbers of vehicles has led to problems faced by everyone on our planet. Car engines use up valuable oil resources. Car exhausts create pollution and contribute to warming the atmosphere above its natural level. Cars in cities create time-wasting congestion. Car crashes result in accident victims on the scale of a continuous war.

If the automobile is to have a future, these are problems which have to be faced and solved.

▽ Having produced best selling family cars, Japanese makers are now concentrating on top level sports machines. Honda aims its NS-X to be a Ferrari-beater, while the Nissan 300ZX is claimed as one of the world's best sports cars.

Nissan 300ZX

Honda NS-X

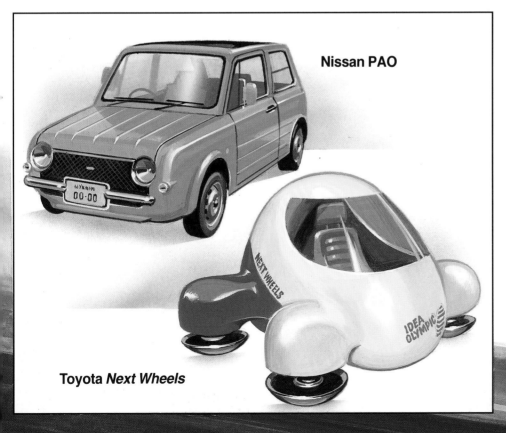

Nissan PAO

Toyota *Next Wheels*

△ Japan's auto firms helped pioneer labor-saving automatic assembly lines. Here, robot machines apply over 1,000 precision welds to each automobile body as it passes down the line.

◁ The Nissan PAO is a limited edition vehicle, produced in small numbers as a "fashion car" for Tokyo trendsetters. The *Next Wheels* was the 1989 winner of Toyota's "Ideas Olympics," an annual competition that encourages weird and wonderful designs.

Future car

In 1987, a streamlined vehicle called *Sunraycer* won an unusual competition, the World Solar Challenge, a 3,000 km (1,187 miles) race across Australia. Like the 22 other entrants, *Sunraycer,* built by General Motors, was powerered by solar cells, which convert the energy in sunlight to electricity. The race was devised by Hans Tholstrup, an Australian who was eager to promote the idea of alternatives to the polluting gasoline engines used by conventional vehicles.

Sunraycer was a spectacular performer, crossing Australia at an average speed of over 65 km/h (41 mph), all on a maximum output from its solar panels of 1,550 watts – about enough to power 25 lightbulbs.

Sunraycer could be the prototype of the sort of cars we will be riding in the early years of the 21st century. Vehicles will certainly be "cleaned up," with non-polluting engines. They may be fueled by petroleum as at present, or by other, cleaner fuels such as methanol, natural gas or even hydrogen. With further development, electric power could be a real winner, especially for driving in cities.

Other future-car features will include computer navigation, control and safety systems including "radar buffers" for use in foggy weather – radar beams will spot traffic ahead in the mist and apply brakes before there is danger of collision.

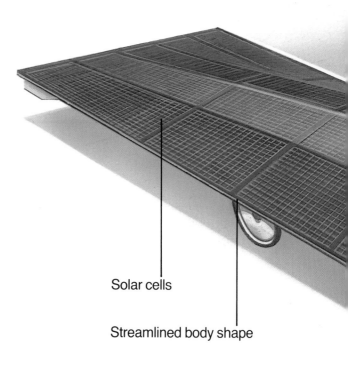

Solar cells

Streamlined body shape

▷ A range of advanced features was built into *Sunraycer.* Its electric motor was a high-tech design weighing just 5 kg (11 lb). The car itself weighed in at 180 kg (397 lb) without the driver. 9,500 solar cells covered the rear half of the car, while a tinted windshield kept the cockpit cool in the blaze of the Australian sun.

Automatic road of the future

This is an idea for an "autoway," tomorrow's highway between cities. Traffic on the autoway is computer controlled and radar buffers keep vehicles a safe distance apart in all weathers. Once on the autoway, a driver turns on the autopilot and relaxes until it's time to take over manual control again.

1 Streamlined vehicles, bodyshapes designed to aid fuel economy.
2 Vehicles made from lightweight materials. Engines run on pollution-free fuels.

3 Automatic trucks share the road with cars and coaches. All vehicles are controlled by their own sensors and computers, together with information picked up from electronic equipment in the road.
4 Landscaping makes up for the trees felled during the highway's construction.
5 Reminder signs tell drivers to switch back to manual control when they leave the autoway. Failure to do so turns on the safety systems. An alarm sounds and power is cut off.

▷ Another competitor in the Solar Challenge was the three-wheeled "Manala." It touched 140 km/h (88 mph) at one point.

Turn indicator lights and rear-view mirror system

Windshield

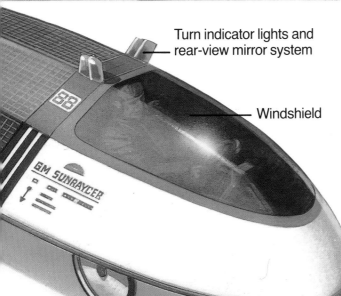

Supercar century

Supercars are generally thought to be vehicles that combine high performance and great looks in about equal quantities. Sadly for most people, a high price tag is usually included too! Here is a group of sporting supercars, each considered to be tops in its time.

△ **1916 Stutz Bearcat.** This was one of the earliest sports cars, with two seats mounted in front of a circular fuel tank. Driver and passenger had to dress warmly, as the cockpit was open to the weather.

◁ **1928 Bentley.** Big and fast, Bentleys won the 24 hour Le Mans race five times from 1924 to 1930. Not everyone was impressed by the big cars' roadholding though. Ettore Bugatti, a rival car maker, once described the Bentley as "the fastest truck in the world."

Rumble seat

△ **1936 Mercedes-Benz 500K Roadster.** The height of 1930s sports luxury, the 500K had swivel spotlights on either side of the windshield, and something you don't see in the 1990s, a rumble seat. This was a back seat for two, which unfolded in front of the twin spare wheels.

▽ **1947 Cisitalia 202 Coupe.** A milestone in car design, the 202 ignored styling features of earlier cars such as long, sweeping mudguards. The 202's bodywork was a smooth one-piece shape, a look followed by car designers ever since.

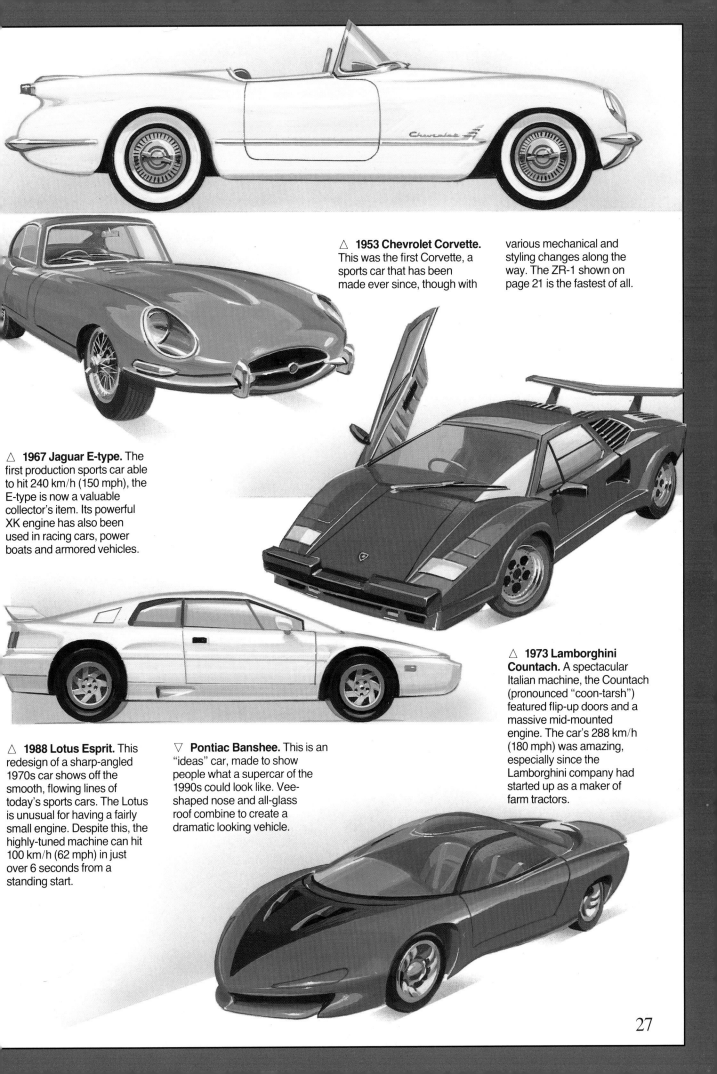

△ **1953 Chevrolet Corvette.** This was the first Corvette, a sports car that has been made ever since, though with various mechanical and styling changes along the way. The ZR-1 shown on page 21 is the fastest of all.

△ **1967 Jaguar E-type.** The first production sports car able to hit 240 km/h (150 mph), the E-type is now a valuable collector's item. Its powerful XK engine has also been used in racing cars, power boats and armored vehicles.

△ **1988 Lotus Esprit.** This redesign of a sharp-angled 1970s car shows off the smooth, flowing lines of today's sports cars. The Lotus is unusual for having a fairly small engine. Despite this, the highly-tuned machine can hit 100 km/h (62 mph) in just over 6 seconds from a standing start.

▽ **Pontiac Banshee.** This is an "ideas" car, made to show people what a supercar of the 1990s could look like. Vee-shaped nose and all-glass roof combine to create a dramatic looking vehicle.

△ **1973 Lamborghini Countach.** A spectacular Italian machine, the Countach (pronounced "coon-tarsh") featured flip-up doors and a massive mid-mounted engine. The car's 288 km/h (180 mph) was amazing, especially since the Lamborghini company had started up as a maker of farm tractors.

27

Facts and records

In the hundred years or so since the invention of the automobile, a fascinating variety of vehicles has taken to the roads. Here are some facts about these cars and the way they have developed. Some ideas that seemed sure-fire winners have failed, others have proved an unexpected success.

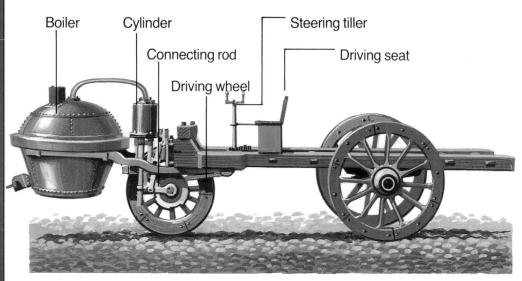

Boiler · Cylinder · Connecting rod · Driving wheel · Steering tiller · Driving seat

Nicholas Cugnot's first steam wagon of 1769 could carry four people, though it was quicker for them to walk. Its top speed was about half walking pace and it had to stop to refuel every few minutes. Cugnot's second carriage, built in 1771, survives to this day in a Paris museum. The picture above shows the various parts of this machine.

In 1824, Londoner Samuel Brown made a powered road vehicle using his invention, the "gas-vacuum engine." This burned gas made from coal. Though capable of climbing hills, the machine was abandoned as it was expensive to run.

▽ Six electric vehicles line up for a recharge in a Paris garage.

The first mechanical vehicle to complete a long journey was Francis Hill's steam coach. In 1840, Hill drove the coach from London to Hastings and back, a distance of 204 km (126 miles). This record stood for over 40 years.

Electric cars were rivals to steam and petroleum-fueled machines in the early days of motoring. The first motor taxis were electric, operated by the London Electric Cab Company between 1897 and 1890. The firm went bust as its cabs were too slow and expensive compared with the horse-drawn cabs of the time.

But electric cars in general were quite popular, often being considered as "ladies cars" because they were quiet and clean. The picture at bottom left shows a group of French electric cars at a recharging station.

For a fee, such stations would recharge your batteries in a few hours or overnight.

Buying fuel was not that easy for pioneer motorists. Few places stocked the "petroleum spirit" used as fuel in early cars. Often, drivers were sold the wrong thing and wondered why their engines would not start. It was not until the 1920s that a widespread system of garages made refueling stops quick and easy. Today, the record for the world's biggest fuel stop is claimed by Little America in Wyoming, which has 52 pumps.

Vehicles and congestion go hand in hand and the means of controlling them appeared quite early. The world's first traffic lights were erected in Detroit, Michigan in 1919. Parking meters took longer though, and it was not until 1935 that the first ones were installed, in Oklahoma City, Oklahoma.

Citroen Traction Avant

Duesenberg Model J

Ford's 1908 Model T "Tin Lizzie" set no new standards in design, but it did break production records and by 1922 more than one million a year were being made. An early Model T cost $850, but by 1925 you could buy one for just $260.

In 1927, Ford brought out the Model A which replaced the T. Today, Ford has a wide range of regularly replaced cars, like other manufacturers.

You had to be rich to afford a Duesenberg Model J. It was produced as a "dream car" and its designers were told not to worry about how much it would cost. The 1928 model was $8,500 just for the chassis – having special bodywork could more than double the price. There were plenty of buyers though, and famous owners included the movie stars Gary Cooper and Clark Gable.

The Citroen Type 7 Traction Avant was a trailblazer of car design. It pioneered both front wheel drive (Traction Avant is French for front drive) and unitary body construction.

Bringing the Type 7 into production was an expensive headache for Citroen, and the firm nearly went bust in the process. The Traction Avant was produced for 23 years, from 1934 to 1957. Its replacement, the Citroen DS, was a futuristic streamlined beauty, nicknamed "the goddess."

The VW Beetle was conceived in 1934 as a cheap to buy "people's car." Production was turned over to military versions for the German forces in World War II. After the war, Ford was offered the car plant, but turned it down. A British Army team got things started again in a Wolfsburg factory and the Volkswagen firm went on to great success.

The Ford Edsel of 1958 holds the record as the biggest flop ever. The car had heavy publicity, but still didn't sell, and Ford lost about $300 million on the car. The Edsel was probably no worse overall than many other cars of the time, but it had one unique feature that became the subject of many jokes – a horseshoe shaped grille, which looked like "it was sucking a lemon." Today, the

Edsel is a rarity that is much sought after by car collectors!

The most fuel-efficient vehicle was built by Tim Leier of the University of Saskatchewan, Canada. In 1968, it covered 9,158 km (5,691 miles) on 4.54 liters (1 gallon) of fuel.

Regular "mileage marathons" are held in many countries, but no entrants have yet beaten Leier's record.

Auto technology

This glossary explains many of the technical terms used in this book.

Anti-lock brake system (ABS)
Braking system that adjusts brake pressure to prevent locked wheels in slippery conditions. In an emergency, many drivers brake too hard, so locking the wheels and creating a dangerous skid. A good ABS senses when the wheels are about to lock and briefly relaxes brake pressure to avoid this.

Chassis
Strong metal or wood backbone structure on which the major parts of a car are attached. Now mostly replaced by unitary or "monocoque" construction in which the body itself acts as a strong, light, rigid box, replacing a separate chassis.

Internal combustion (IC) engine
Engine in which fuel is burned inside the engine structure rather than, say, a steam engine, where fuel is burned outside a water-filled boiler to produce heated steam.

The type of IC engine used in almost all automobiles is the four-stroke system. Here, power is produced during four up-and-down strokes of a piston in a cylinder. The diagram shows the four strokes in action – intake, compression, power and exhaust.

Engines can vary in the number of cylinders they have. Most ordinary cars have four-cylinder engines. Luxury and high-performance models can have 5, 6, 8, 12 or even 16 cylinders. Generally speaking, the more cylinders an engine has, the smoother it is and the more power it produces.

The number of valves varies too. Many modern engines have four valves per cylinder, increasing the efficiency of the intake and exhaust system. Ideally, a four valve design gives both extra power and better fuel economy.

Petroleum
Mineral oil, used as the basis for fuel in auto engines. Raw petroleum is green, brown or black when first pumped out of the earth. This thick

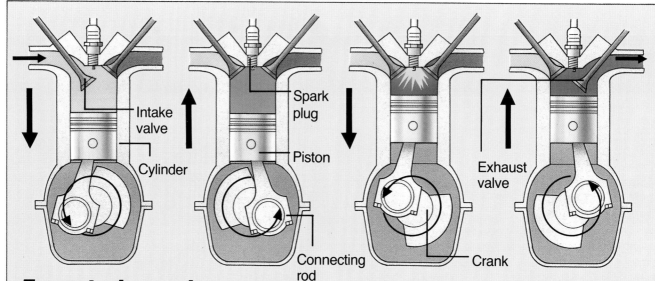

Four stroke cycle

1 Intake stroke
Piston moves down cylinder. Fuel and air drawn in top of cylinder through intake valve.

2 Compression stroke
Piston moves up cylinder, squashing the fuel-air mixture. Both valves closed.

3 Power stroke
Mixture ignited by an electric spark from the spark plug. Explosion forces piston down cylinder.

4 Exhaust stroke
Piston moves back up, pushing waste gases out of the open exhaust valve. Four-stroke cycle now repeats.

The up-and-down piston action is converted into a turning movement by the connecting rod and crank. The crank is joined to the wheels by a system of gears and shafts.

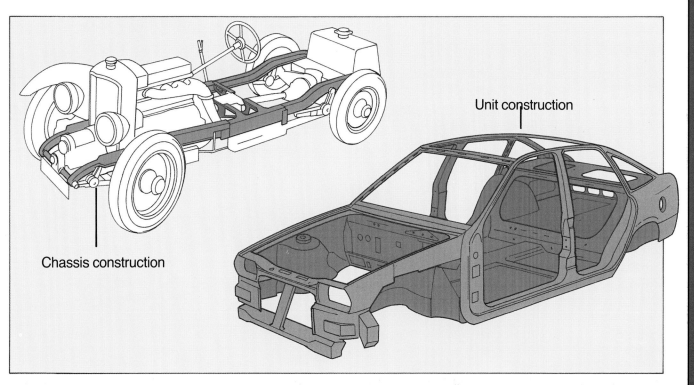

Unit construction

Chassis construction

crude oil is refined to produce different grades of oil product including motor spirit (gasoline) for cars and diesel oil for trucks.

Pollution
Pollution caused by automobiles is mostly in the form of substances given out with exhaust fumes. One such is lead. When mixed with fuel, it acts as a lubricant, reducing wear and tear in the engine. However, lead is poisonous, so lead-free fuel can be made as an answer to this problem.

Other poisons can be removed using a catalytic converter. This is a device fitted to the exhaust system which uses a substance (such as platinum) called a catalyst to remove some of the harmful gases.

Production line
System for producing cars, pioneered by

Henry Ford. A production line consists of a moving conveyor belt on which vehicles are carried. At various points along the way, groups of assembly workers add on the different parts until, at the end of the line, finished cars can be started and driven off for testing before being delivered to customers.

On a modern line, robot equipment is used for much of the assembly, including welding and painting.

Streamlined
An object that is shaped to pass through the air at speed with as little resistance as possible. Put simply, smooth rounded shapes push through air more easily

than square ones. In a car, this means that less power is needed for high performance, so less fuel is needed.

Supersonic
Faster than the speed of sound. At sea level this is about 1,226 km/h (762 mph), falling with height to 1,062 km/h (660 mph) above 12 km (7.45 miles) altitude.

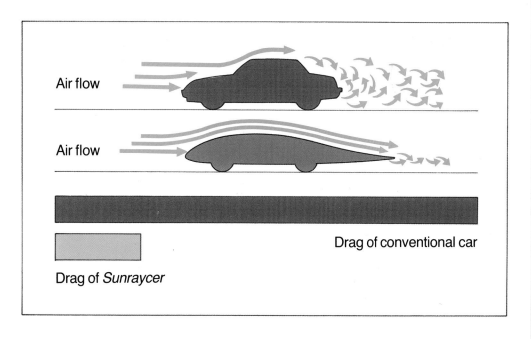

Air flow

Air flow

Drag of conventional car

Drag of *Sunraycer*

Index